CHIP CARVING
Techniques & Patterns

CHIP CARVING
Techniques & Patterns

Wayne Barton

Sterling Publishing Co. Inc. New York

Library of Congress Cataloging in Publication Data

Barton, Wayne.
    Chip carving

    Includes index.
    1. Wood-carving.   2. Wood-carving—Patterns.
I. Title.
TT199.7.B37   1984   736′.4   84-8779
ISBN 0-8069-7924-0 (pbk.)

              5   7   9   10   8   6

Published by Sterling Publishing Co., Inc.
Two Park Avenue, New York, N.Y. 10016
Distributed in Australia by Oak Tree Press Co., Ltd.
P.O. Box K514 Haymarket, Sydney 2000, N.S.W.
Distributed in the United Kingdom by Blandford Press
Link House, West Street, Poole, Dorset BH15 1LL, England
Distributed in Canada by Oak Tree Press Ltd.
℅ Canadian Manda Group, P.O. Box 920, Station U
Toronto, Ontario, Canada M8Z 5P9
Manufactured in the United States of America

This book is lovingly dedicated to my wife, Marlies, and her parents, Paul and Marie Bernhard-Hartmann of Hinwil, Switzerland.

CONTENTS

A note about the photographs:
It is very difficult to photographically reproduce some of the subtleties of chip carving. Because there is no point of reference when the camera views the carving straight on, sometimes a false impression—an optical illusion—is created and it appears that the design or letter that is carved *into* the wood is raised from it. The deeper the carving, the more likely this is to occur.

PREFACE

As a very small child, I sat at my grandfather's knee and watched him do magical and wonderful things to pieces of wood with his pocket knife. Then one day he called me to his side and put a pocket knife of my very own in my hand, I was thrilled, I was five years old and I was about to fall in love forever.

Woodcarving allows an artist to work and commune with nature in a very special way. Unlike other artists, a woodcarver does not create his medium of expression. Nature has already done that for him. His genius is the ability to visualize the completed work within the wood itself before he starts, and then hold that vision ever-constant as he physically recreates what he has already seen in his mind's eye.

Wood affords the carver an opportunity to take a natural life-form of endless variation and transform it into the permanent voice of his own vision. Because of the unique qualities of wood, it becomes a most persuasive and compelling orator.

The woodcarver gives his strength, patience, care, and devotion to Mother Nature. She gives him her charm, beauty, warmth, and eternity. That's love.

INTRODUCTION

Various forms of chip carving have been practiced in virtually every culture and civilization throughout time. This includes prehistoric civilizations, although survival of wood artifacts from this period are extremely rare. Archeologists suggest that some of the surviving stone carvings are similar to work that was executed in wood. The reason for this popularity may be found in the simplicity of tools used in chip carving and its endless variety of fascinating motifs.

What is chip carving anyway? "Chip carving" describes that form of carving that incises a pattern or design directly into wood. Chip carving gets its name from the technique employed, namely, removing a series of precise, regular chips of wood to form an engraved design lower than the surface of the wood. In other words, the wood that is removed leaves exactly the design desired, as opposed to removing shavings to extract a form or design from the wood as in relief and in-the-round carving (whittling).

Chip carving as we know it today originated in Europe. In the last few centuries there has been such an exchange of motifs between countries that the national origin of particular designs is quite obscure. In Germany and Switzerland chip carving is known as Kerbschnitzen which means "engraving carving." In Switzerland, as in other European countries, Kerbschnitzen was originally a peasant art. It was used to decorate every wooden tool, piece of furniture and utensil around the house and barn . . . and the house and barn. Everything—water buckets, breadboards, spoons, milking stools, cupboards—was carved.

Chip carving has sometimes been viewed by the uninitiated and unknowledgeable as an inferior style of woodcarving to be tolerated only as a learning device for beginners that teaches patience, control, and discipline. It does teach all of this . . . and more. But chip carving is an art in a class of its own. It is currently enjoying a renaissance and is once again being recognized for the true art form that it is.

Today, chip carving still can be applied to more kinds of surfaces than any other kind of carving. It flourishes in the mountain valleys of Switzerland. The Swiss method of chip carving which is illustrated and explained in this book maintains the wonderful, traditional simplicity of its origins, both in the tools used and the motifs.

This book is a step-by-step explanation of a method of chip carving that will bring hours of pleasure and satisfaction to both the beginning and experienced woodcarver alike. Both will discover that pleasing and impressive results can be achieved in a very short period of time.

Should the reader have any questions or like to make comments, you are invited to contact the author through the publisher.

SELECTION OF WOOD

Nearly all types of wood can be used, for chip carving, but some will serve far better than others. There are four criteria important to the chip carver that will guide him in making the best selection for his purpose.

First is the hardness of the wood. Because this is a one-handed effort, unlike chisel carving, and is done without the aid of a mallet, the softer woods will allow you more control. Less pressure while carving will let you concentrate on applying smooth, flowing cuts to your design. It is also less tiring. If, however, you are creating furniture or a cutting board, you will require a harder wood, in which case it is best not to create a deep-cut design. But wood that is too soft will crush and tear even beneath a sharp knife.

Second is the tightness of the grain. Generally, the tighter and straighter the grain the better. Open-grain woods, such as mahogany, have a tendency to split and will severely limit the intricacy of any pattern. Irregularly grained woods will lessen your control when cutting, making accuracy more difficult.

Third is the type of grain in the wood. The more spectacular and exotic the grain, such as that found in South American and African woods, the more it will compete with your work. You will get the most satisfactory results with unspectacular, straight-grained woods.

Fourth is the color of the wood. Light-colored woods give a better contrast of the shadow and light that emphasizes the carving. Dark-colored woods and stained woods tend to obscure this light-shadow effect. If your carving is to make only a muted statement in the overall work as is done with some furniture, dark-colored woods, either natural or stained, will serve nicely.

The queen of all woods for chip carving, that best meets these four criteria, is universal and known by various names. In the United States it is called basswood or linden. In the United Kingdom it is known as lime or limewood. In Germanic-speaking countries it is called Lindenholz. In the United States northern-grown basswood is tighter-grained and harder than the southern-grown and is more usually dependable when doing intricate carving.

There are several types of poplar that will run a close second to basswood for workability and color. There are also a variety of pines that lend themselves very well to chip carving because of their grain, color, and density. Pine has the distinction of being a construction wood used in cabinets, doors, and furniture, broadening your application of chip carving. But basswood will give you your greatest delight for just pure carving pleasure. It will allow a high degree of control when cutting both with and across the grain. If basswood is used in any construction, such as in boxes, you will find it usually quite free of warping.

One last word on wood. You will have better results if your wood is not too dry. Dry wood tends to split and crack as you carve. Basswood carves very nicely with a 9 to 12 percent moisture content.

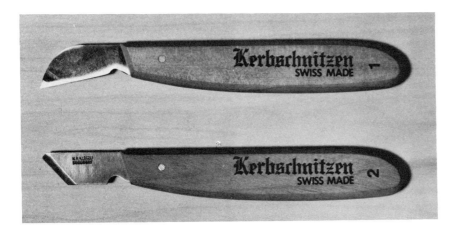

Illus. 1. Swiss chip carving knives.

TOOLS

In the past chip carving has been performed with quite a variety of cutting implements. Though there are many knives available today, the Swiss method of chip carving requires the use of only two, both of which are designed specifically for that method of carving. How these knives are used has determined three important factors in their construction: the steel, the handle, and shape of the blade.

The steel is a high quality not given to rusting. It is well tempered to hold its cutting edge, yet not brittle. The blade is thick enough so it is not overly flexible and will not snap under pressure.

The handle is comfortable and shaped to fit firmly in your hand. Some knives have thin handles that are shaped round or oval and have a tendency to turn in your hand while carving because they are hard to hold on to. This becomes fatiguing and frustrating.

The most important factor is the shape of the blade and its size. If the cutting edge does not strike the work at the correct angle when your hand is in a natural and comfortable position, your carving will become difficult to execute.

The two Swiss chip carving knives used by the author for all the work illustrated in this book are quite different from each other in design, function, and use. (Illus. 1) The most frequently used is the cutting knife. It is used to make all cuts both straight and curved. The other is called a stab knife. It is never used for cutting. Rather, it is used only to indent or impress a mark in the wood to create or enhance a design. However, this function is an important one.

The other tools you need are as simple as the knives you will use. They are a soft lead pencil (a grade "B" 0.5mm in a mechanical pencil will do well), an accurate mechanical compass with a soft lead that will give you true circles, a good straightedge and ruler, and an eraser. The measurements found in this book are in both metric units and inches but because of its simplicity, the metric system is given preference. Rulers incremented in both systems are readily available.

SHARPENING

There are as many products on the market today for sharpening tools as there are methods of sharpening. There is also no such thing as an absolute one-and-only right way to sharpen a knife. You may already have a method that works very well for you. If so, use it. What is important is that your knife is truly sharp and at the correct angle. When carving, there is absolutely no substitute for a truly sharp blade. Without it, you will never realize your full potential as a carver.

Here is an excellent and simple method of getting a perfectly sharp edge at the correct angle on your chip carving knives. You will need two sharpening stones, a medium-grade India and a hard Arkansas. Be sure the Arkansas is a hard grade and not soft. You can tell by running your thumb over the surface. If it feels a bit gritty it's a soft grade, no matter what the label reads. A good hard Arkansas will feel almost glass smooth to the touch. Quality in hard Arkansas stones is not determined by color with some good grades having both black and white within the same stone.

There are two criteria for your choice of stones. One is that they

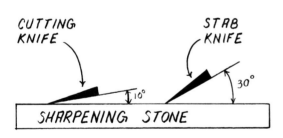
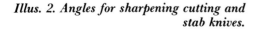

Illus. 2. Angles for sharpening cutting and stab knives.

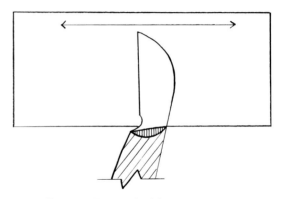

Illus. 3. Slide both sides of blade back and forth across stone to sharpen.

must be absolutely flat. You can determine this by taking a true straightedge and placing it across the surface of the stone in both directions. If any light appears under the straightedge, particularly in the middle, the stone is "dished" and if used, will round the tip of the knife. This is exactly what you don't want to have happen. To be sure the stone is absolutely flat, no light should show under the straightedge. The other criterion is that the stone be large enough to accommodate the entire cutting edge of the knife at once. Otherwise you will have extreme difficulty getting a smooth, straight cutting edge.

When sharpening either knife use a light-weight oil made specifically for this purpose. Smooth it on the stones as you work. It will prevent them from clogging with metal particles and it will help float the blade, making sharpening easier. Because the cutting knife is used most in chip carving, let us sharpen it first. Begin by placing the India stone on a firm, flat surface. Put the blade flat on the stone and raise it on its edge approximately 10 degrees. If you sharpen it much more than 10 degrees, you will cause a "thickness" behind the edge, particularly at the tip of the blade. Your edge may be sharp, but this "thickness" will cause the knife to drag through the wood. Concentrate on putting more pressure on the heel of the blade rather than the tip. This will help prevent rounding the tip. A back and forth movement with pressure on one side, and then equally on the other, will do nicely. This method will make the blade sharp without causing a heavy burr. Creating a heavy burr will only remove more metal from the blade than is necessary. It will also make the process of sharpening longer and more laborious. (Illus. 2 and 3)

Check for a burr by running your finger across the flat of the blade on either side towards the edge. If you feel a drag or scraping on your finger, you have a burr. This can be eliminated by continuing to sharpen in the same manner, but with less pressure. Work the burr from one side to the other until it finally disappears or falls off.

You will know your knife is sharp and ready for final honing when there is no burr, and you can see no light reflecting off the edge. Check light reflection by holding the knife under a strong light with your finger on the tip of the blade. Sight the blade from approximately a 45 degree angle and rock it from side to side. If no light reflects from the edge, you are ready for final honing. The only reason light will ever reflect from the edge, even with the faintest thin line, is because it is still rounded.

For final honing take the hard Arkansas stone and use it exactly as you did the India stone. The hard Arkansas will polish the metal so the blade will glide through the wood rather than drag. Be careful that you hone equally on each side so that you do not create a burr. Your blade can be sharp, but if it has any hint of a burr it will drag through the wood and can cause a crushing or tearing in any soft spots the wood may have.

When you feel you've finished sharpening your knife, give it one final check for the reflection of light. You can check for drag caused by a burr, thickness behind the edge, or incomplete sharpness by cutting diagonally across the grain of a scrap piece of wood. Your knife should flow smoothly and steadily. If it doesn't, check the three causes of drag mentioned above.

Under normal use, you will need to freshen up your edge periodically only on the hard Arkansas stone. You will know when this is necessary because you will find yourself using more pressure to get the same results you did initially. Also, light will reflect from the edge. Frequency of sharpening will depend on the quality of steel in your blade, variety of wood being used (some are more gritty than others, dulling the blade faster), and type of cuts being made (deeper and curved cuts wear an edge more quickly).

To sharpen the stab knife use precisely the same stones and procedure as you did with the cutting knife, with one exception. Because the stab knife is used only for impressing or indenting the wood to enhance a design, the angle of the cutting edge is more crucial than its sharpness. With the stab knife you will want to keep the thickness behind the edge. In order to do this, sharpen the stab knife at approximately a 30 degree angle. This is the only difference in sharpening procedure between the two knives.

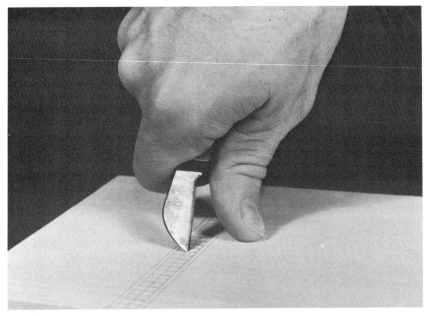

Illus. 4. Correct way to hold the cutting knife in the first position.

HOW TO HOLD THE KNIVES

Many carvers will tell you that, "A carver is only as good as the tools he uses." The second half of this truism should be, "and how he uses them." Holding and using the knives in the correct manner will make your carving infinitely easier, faster, and more pleasant.

There are two positions for the cutting knife. For the first position, hold the knife in your right hand and place the first joint of your thumb (curved outwards) at the end of the handle by the blade on the lower inside ridge of the handle. Wrap the rest of your fingers around the handle. (Left handed carvers, like the author, simply reverse this process.) Your thumb and knuckles will rest on your work, guiding and supporting the blade as though it was a sixth digit. Never try using the cutting knife without some part of your hand or a finger touching your work as a guide, or you will have no control. Your thumb should never leave the handle while cutting, as it might when peeling potatoes. (Illus. 4)

Illus. 5. Correct way to hold cutting knife in second position.

The second position is achieved by moving the thumb directly on top of the spine of the handle with the first knuckle of the thumb still next to the blade, not on it. These two positions will give you the proper (and same) angle for carving in opposing directions. Held properly and consistently, your blade will always be in the wood at the correct angle. (Illus. 5)

The first position is used for all line cuts, both straight and curved. It is also used for the first and third cuts of small regular triangular chips. When using the first position, turn your wrist away from your body. The second position is used only for the second cut of the same triangular chips. (See p. 22) It is much easier and you will have much more control if, when you are making line cuts or larger curved chips in the first position, to simply keep turning your work rather than keep changing positions.

The stab knife is held with one or two hands perpendicular to your work. It is thrust downwards to make an impression of the desired depth and length of indentation. (Illus. 6)

When carving, keep your elbow close to your body. This will give you added leverage and strength from your shoulder. Also, do all of your work in your lap (which means you get to sit down) unless your piece is too large to hold. To sit and work on a table or bench is to forfeit your leverage and strength.

Illus. 6. Correct way to hold the stab knife.

These positions may seem awkward at first, but with practice they will become quite natural to you. Ideally, you should never go back over a cut once it is made. A single cut at the correct depth and angle should suffice. This will give your work a very clean and crisp appearance. If your angle is too shallow, you will not have the right depth for the contrast of light and shadow. If your angle is too deep, it will become difficult to get a clean, crisp cut. (Illus. 7) Remember, what you are trying to achieve is a good contrast between light and shadow. In order to help you do this, carve with a strong light, either natural or artificial. You will be able to determine the end result better as you work. Also, it will be less tiring for your eyes.

One final word on holding the cutting knife that may prove helpful: After you have been carving a while, you may find the ridge your thumb rests on in the first position a bit uncomfortable. If so, simply round it off slightly by sanding at the point at which your thumb rests. You should be able to carve for hours without it ever bothering you.

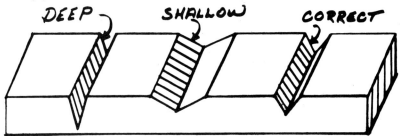

Illus. 7. Correct angle for cutting wood.

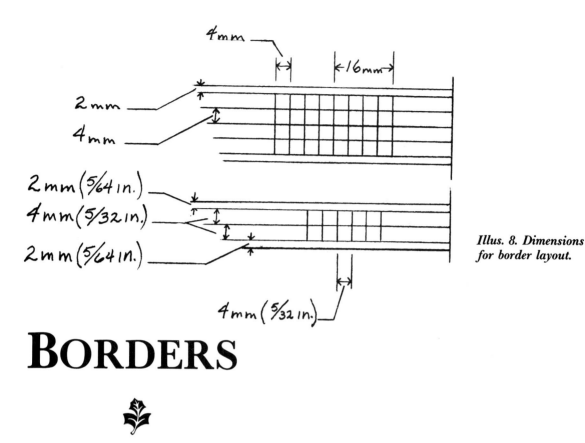

Illus. 8. Dimensions for border layout.

BORDERS

The triangular chip. A number of borders may be made based on the triangular chip. The layout for these borders is quite simple as they are based on a row (or rows) of squares, 4 mm on each side. (Illus. 8) It will make your practice easy if you lay your work on boards 12 in. long, by 4–6 in. wide, by a minimum of ⅜ in. thick. This size board is easy to handle and can be carved on both sides.

To begin, hold the cutting knife in the first position. (Illus. 8A) Place the tip at the corner of a square and raise the blade up so that it forms a "V" on the wood. Thrust straight down to the opposite corner of that square. In the first position, your thumb should always be on your work. (Illus. 9)

Now switch the cutting knife to the second position and place the tip at the same corner as you did originally. You are now going to make an identical cut in the opposite direction in the square next to your original square. Turning your work slightly, thrust down to the opposite corner of the square. In the second position, the knuckle of your first finger should always rest on your work. (Illus. 10)

For the third cut which frees the chip completely, switch the knife

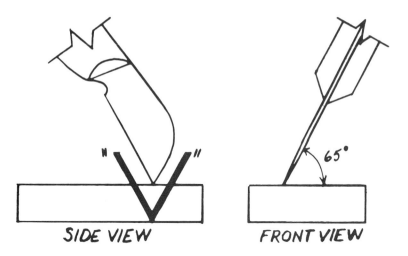

Illus. 8A. Correct angle for cutting knife for making triangular chip.

back to the first position. Place the tip of the blade on the uncut side of the chip with the blade edge parallel to your last cut. In one motion, pull the knife towards you along the uncut side, simultaneously pressing down until you have run along the entire third side. If executed correctly, the chip will pop right out. Upon examination, you will also notice that the three sides of your cut have automatically met in the middle at the bottom of your cut. (Illus. 11–15)

The curved chip. The curved chip is made in two cuts in the first position. Make your first cut on the line. The second cut will make a crescent-shaped chip. Always take care not to insert the blade any deeper than necessary to remove the chip. To do so will increase the risk of undercutting your work—lifting out sections you intended to keep. Also, whenever possible, make the first cut of a new chip away from the work you have already completed. This, too, will help prevent losing sections you want to keep. Remember, when cutting curves or circles, that the smaller the radius the higher you should raise the knife on its tip. Doing this will leave only a minimum of blade in the wood, allowing you to make smooth and clean curved cuts.

The straight line chip. Straight line cuts or chips are generally used to create certain borders, as accents around borders and designs, and to establish grids. They are cut freehand in the first position only, without the aid of a straightedge. To cut a straight line, keep your hand firmly on your work and move along steadily. Train your eye to look directly in front of the blade while you are cutting. Do not look at where the blade is in the wood or where it has just been. Your eye will direct your hand where to go.

The positions and methods of carving borders are applied to all other chip carving. Practicing carving the various borders will sharpen your skills.

When laying out borders on specific pieces, such as the top of a box, it is best to first establish the center lines equally dividing your work into four sections. Measure 12 mm in from the outside edge of the piece and then start marking for the lines of the border. With most pieces, unless they are very small, this dimension will not have your border looking as though it is falling off the edge and will still give room for any further design you may desire within the border. Once the border lines are drawn, measure from the center outwards on all four sides when you begin the actual border layout, whichever one you may choose. This will insure that your border and design will be even on all sides. (Illus. 13–21)

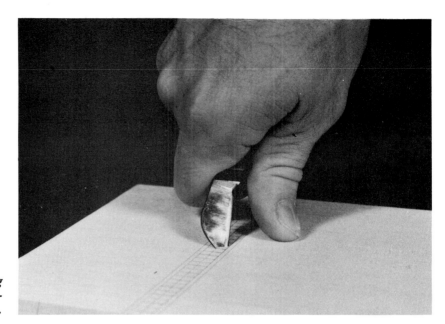

Illus. 9. Executing first cut in first position.

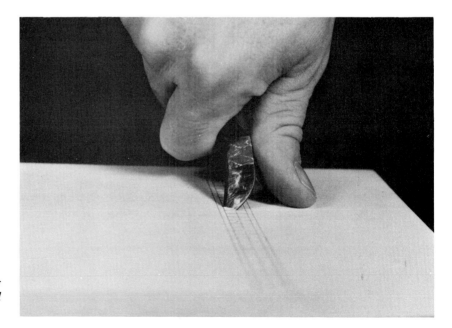

Illus. 10. Executing second cut in second position.

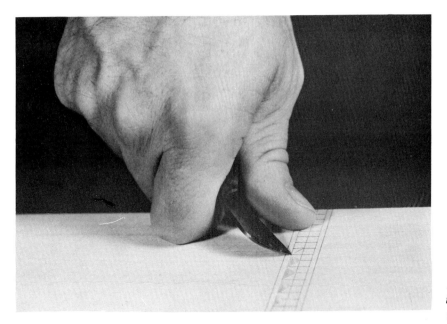

Illus. 11. Starting third cut in first position.

Illus. 12. Executing third cut.

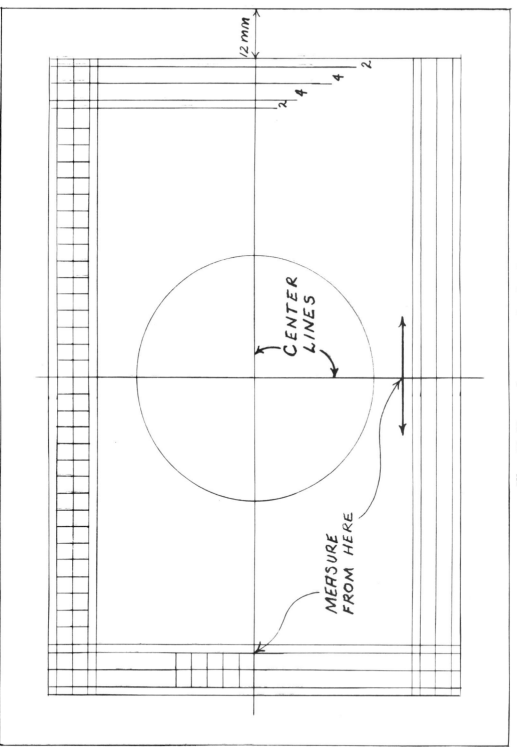

Illus. 13. How to lay out complete border.

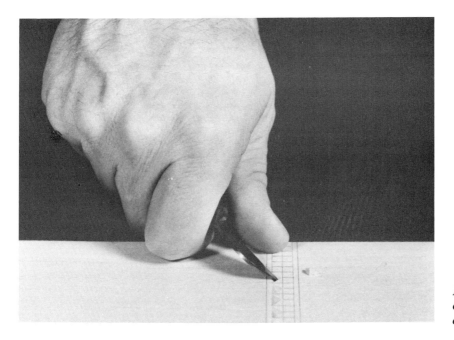

Illus. 14. Completion of third cut relieving chip.

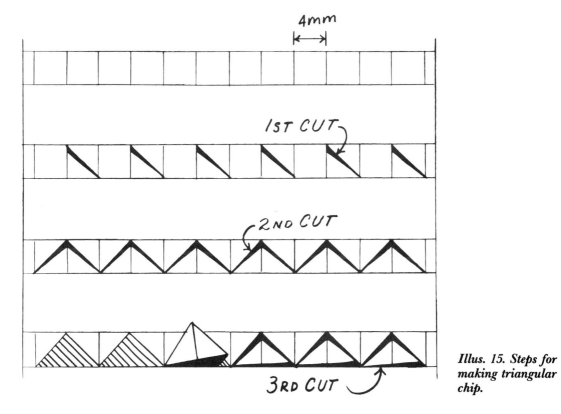

4mm

1ST CUT

2ND CUT

3RD CUT

Illus. 15. Steps for making triangular chip.

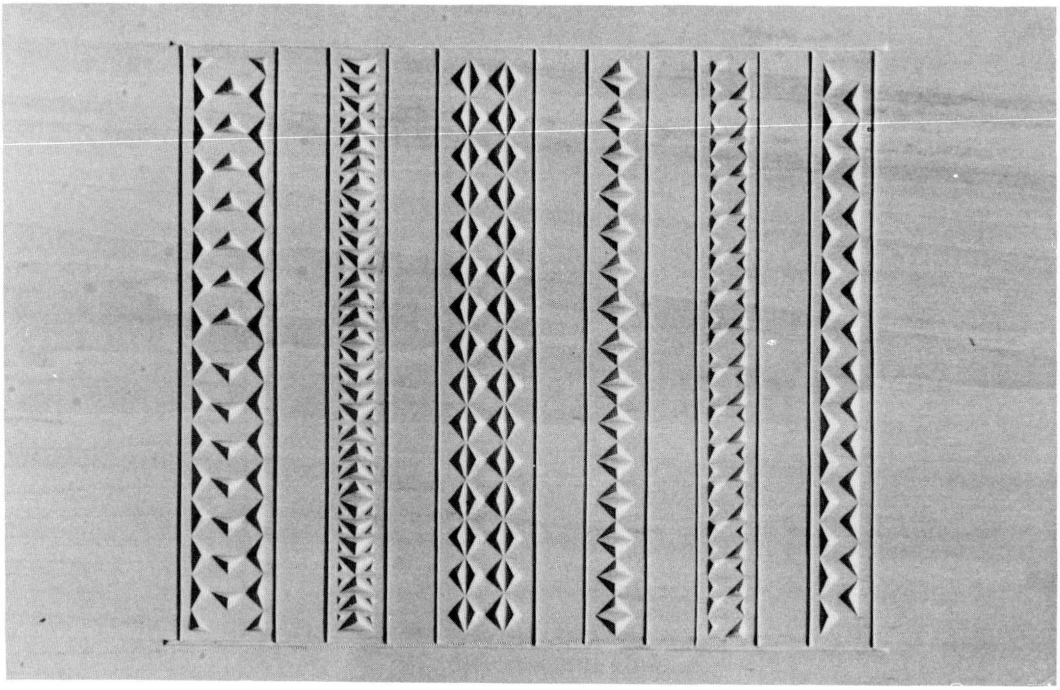

Illus. 17

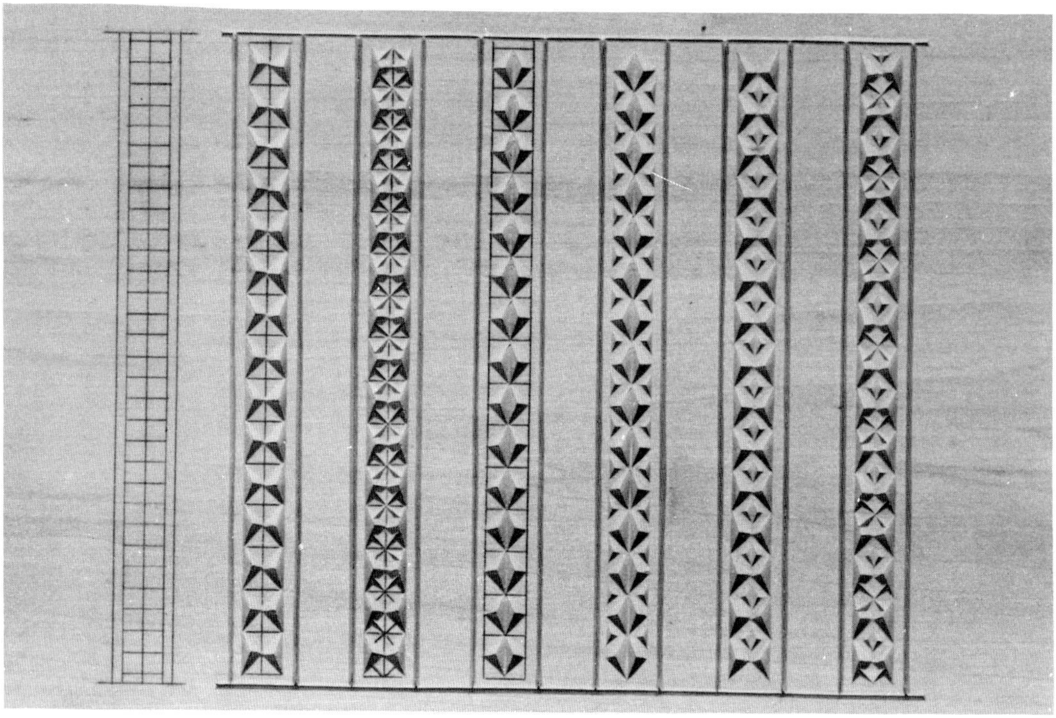

Illus. 16

CUT ON DOTTED LINES

←3CM.→

Illus. 18

Illus. 19

GRIDS

There are occasions when you may want to cover larger areas such as panels on doors and cabinets, or on boxes with a design. This can be accomplished simply with intersecting lines that form a design of squares and diamonds. It can also be an elaborate motif repeated to form a large overall design. These are called grids.

You will find when creating a grid design that the stab knife can be quite useful. By pressing into the wood with the stab knife, it can create its own design that will certainly enhance the appearance of the finished carving. The stab knife complements your cutting knife very well.

When cutting a grid of intersecting straight lines (or any other lines), practice doing it freehand. Never use a straightedge. If the straightedge should move, you will lose control and ruin your carving. (Illus. 22–33)

34 GRIDS

Illus. 26

Illus. 25

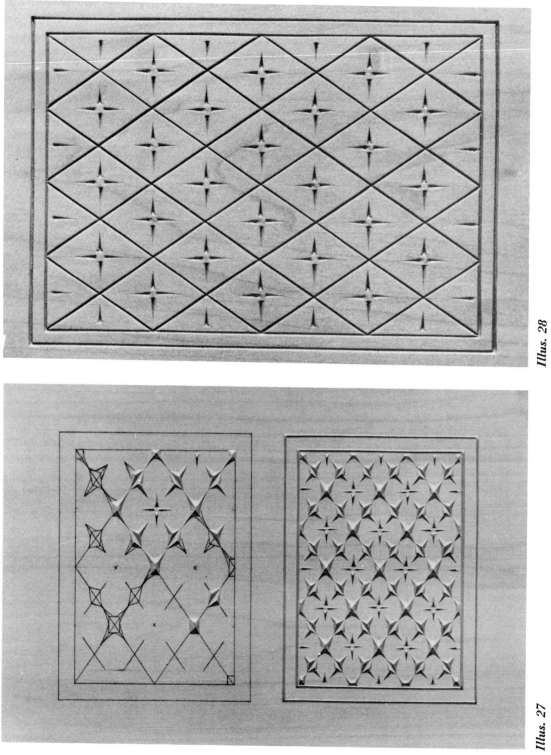

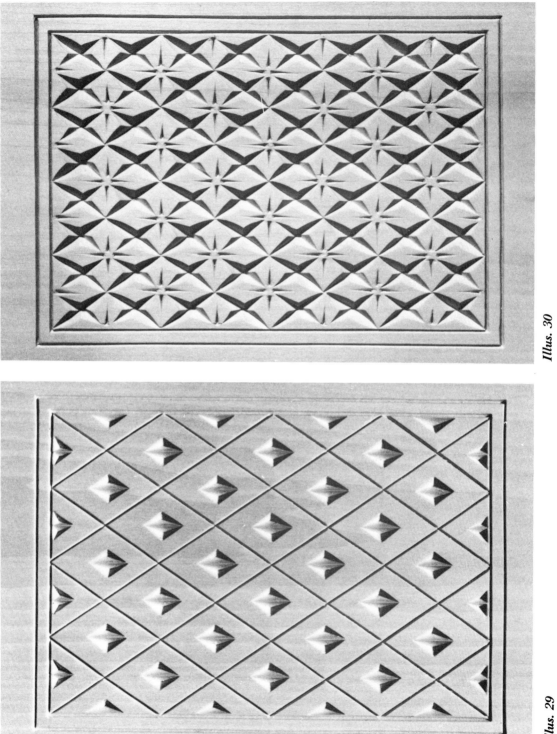

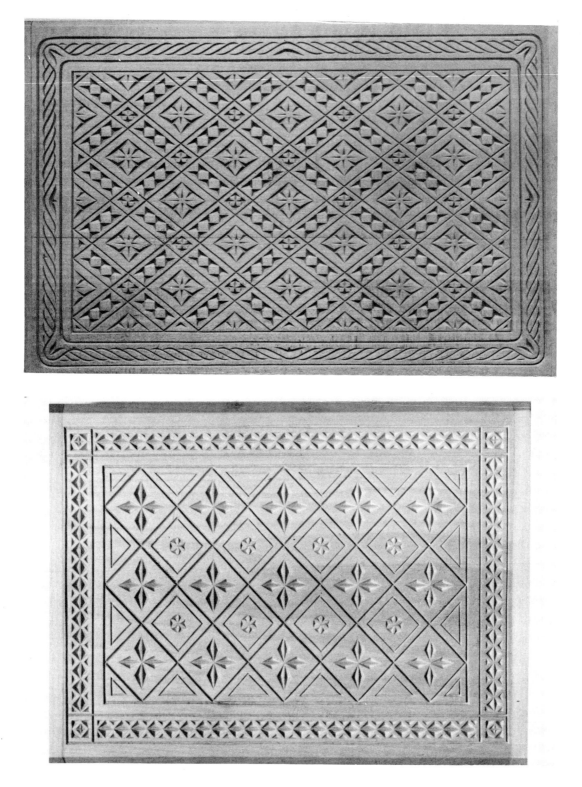

Illus. 32

Illus. 31

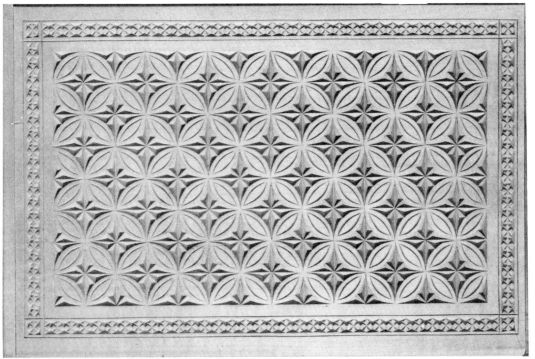

ROSETTES

Creating rosettes is one of the most enjoyable aspects of chip carving. It will afford you endless opportunities for artistic expression. In many instances a single design will provide two rosettes. Simply by carving the reverse or opposite of the original, you will get what is sometimes called the positive and negative from one rosette pattern. (Illus. 38–40)

An excellent way to start making rosettes is by overlapping a series of circles. (Illus. 41)

1. Draw a straight line. Place the compass at point 1 and draw a complete circle. Make circles of the same size at the intersection of the line and the original circle, points 2 and 3.
2. Place the compass at points 4, 5, 6, and 7, and continue to draw full circles.
3. Points 8 through 19 will draw partial circles, filling in the design. Finish by hand drawing the outer lines, as illustrated, between points 8 and 9.

Circles that are divided equally by different numbers each produce their own style of rosette. Though a circle technically does not

*Illus. 35–37. Knotty
pine cabinet doors
showing positive and
negative rosettes.*

have sides, rosettes are commonly referred to as having them. The following geometrical formulas for dividing a circle are done only with a good mechanical compass and a straightedge. It is really quite easy.

Illus. 38. Positive and negative rosettes from the same design.

Illus. 39. Positive and negative rosettes.

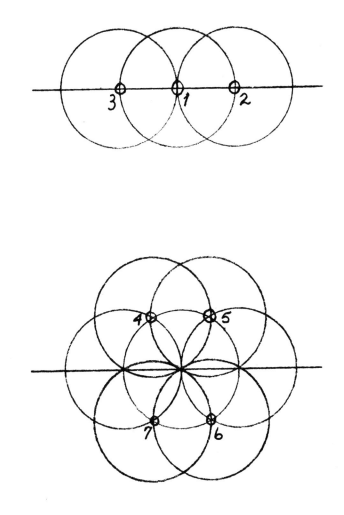

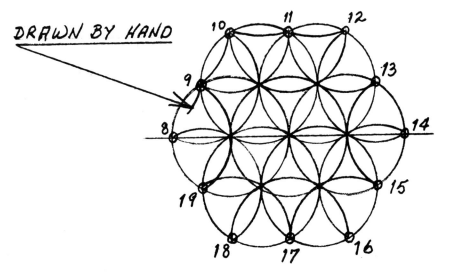

DRAWN BY HAND

Illus. 40. Making a rosette.

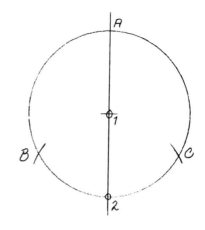

Illus. 41

The three-sided rosette (Illus. 41)

1. Draw a vertical line.
2. Make a circle at point 1.
3. Place compass at point 2 and strike points *B* and *C*.
4. Points *A*, *B*, and *C* form an equilateral triangle. (Illus. 42)

Illus. 42

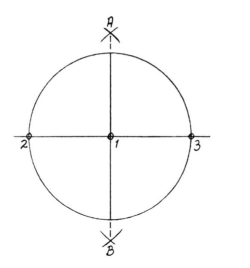

Illus. 43

The four-sided rosette (Illus. 43)

1. Draw a horizontal line.
2. Make a circle at point 1.
3. Open compass larger than original radius. Set new compass opening at points 1 and 2 and strike intersections establishing points *A* and *B*.
4. Line drawn from points *A* and *B* will bisect original line forming right angles and divide circle into four equal parts. (Illus. 44)

Illus. 44

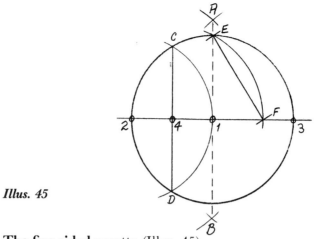

Illus. 45

The five-sided rosette (Illus. 45)

1. Draw a horizontal line.
2. Make a circle at point 1.
3. Using the same compass opening, set compass at point 2 and draw semicircle establishing points *C* and *D*.
4. Draw line between *C* and *D* establishing point 4.
5. Bisect original line as in the four-sided rosette establishing point *E*.
6. Set compass opening from point 4 to point *E* and draw arch *E-F*.
7. Set compass opening at *E-F*. This will divide the circle into five equal parts. (Illus. 46)

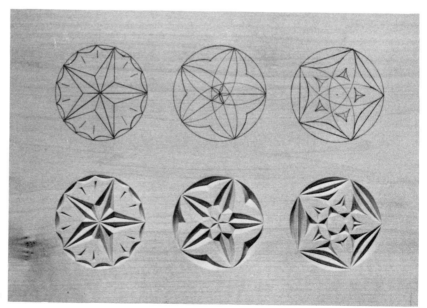

Illus. 46

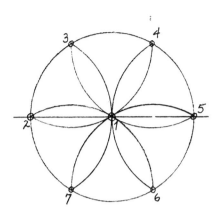

Illus. 47

The six-sided rosette (Illus. 47)
1. Draw a horizontal line.
2. Make a circle at point 1.
3. Using the same compass opening, set compass at point 2 and strike points 3 and 7.
4. Set compass at point 3 and repeat until you return to point 2. (Illus. 48)

Illus. 48

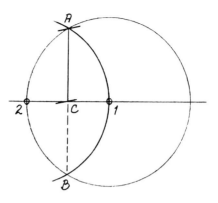

Illus. 49

The seven-sided rosette (Illus. 49)

1. Draw a horizontal line.
2. Make a circle at point 1.
3. Using the same compass opening, set compass at point 2 and strike points *A* and *B*.
4. Set the compass opening at *A-C*. This will divide the circle into seven equal parts. (Illus. 50)

Illus. 50

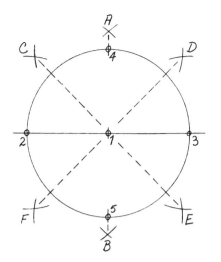

Illus. 51

The eight-sided rosette (Illus. 51)

1. Draw a horizontal line.
2. Make a circle at point 1.
3. Bisect original line as in the four-sided rosette establishing points 4 and 5.
4. Reduce compass opening and set compass at point 2 striking between 2-*A* and 2-*B*. Repeat at points 3, 4, and 5. This will establish intersections *C, D, E,* and *F*.
5. Lines drawn from *C-E* and *D-F* will complete the division of the circle into eight equal parts. (Illus. 52)

Illus. 52

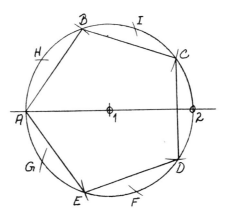

Illus. 53

The ten-sided rosette (Illus. 53)
1. Draw a horizontal line.
2. Make a circle at point 1.
3. Repeat procedure for five-sided rosette establishing points *A*, *B*, *C*, *D*, and *E*.
4. Using the same compass opening, set compass at point 2 and repeat step 3 establishing points *F*, *G*, *H*, and *I*. This will complete the division of the circle into 10 equal parts. (Illus. 54)

Illus. 54

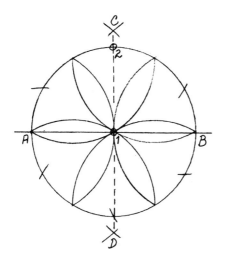

Illus. 55

The twelve-sided rosette (Illus. 55)

1. Repeat procedure for six-sided rosette.
2. Bisect line *A-B* establishing line *C-D.*
3. Using the same compass opening set compass at point 2 and repeat step 1. This will complete the division of the circle into 12
   equal parts. (Illus. 56–77)

Illus. 56

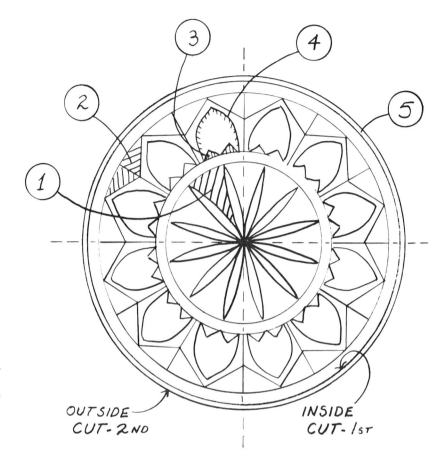

Illus. 57. Order of removing chips from design. Take out largest first.

OUTSIDE CUT-2ND

INSIDE CUT-1ST

Illus. 58. Extracting carving from design.

Illus. 59. Chair back.

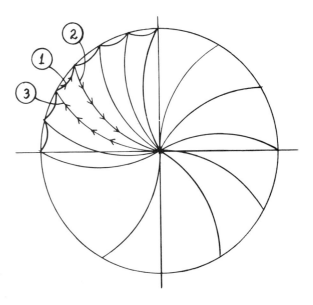

Illus. 60. Order and direction of cuts for extracting curved triangular chip from swirl design.

Illus. 61. Swirl.

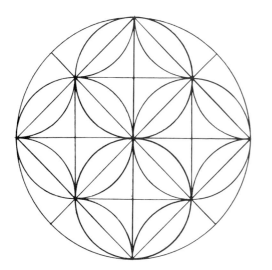

Illus. 62

Illus. 63

Illus. 64

Illus. 65

Illus. 66. Compass rose.

Illus. 67

Illus. 68

Illus. 69

Illus. 70

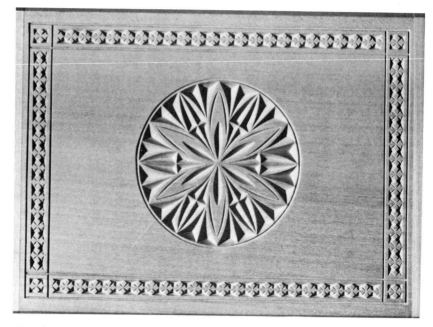

Illus. 71

Illus. 72

Illus. 73

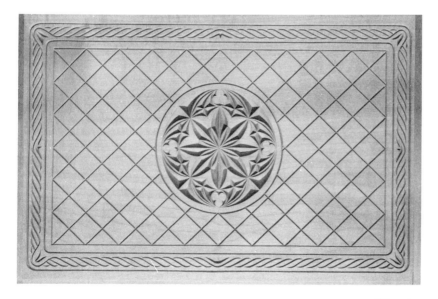

Illus. 74

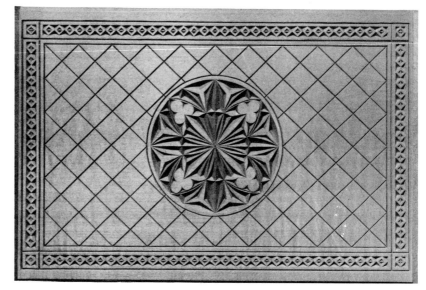

Illus. 75

Illus. 76

Illus. 77.

Illus. 78

Illus. 79. A bud de-sign.

FREE-FORM

One of the delightful aspects of chip carving is that this particular technique goes beyond the boundaries of geometric design. There are many forms found in nature that lend themselves well to chip carving. Flowers, foliage, birds, animals, and even scenery give another dimension to chip carving.

Free-form designs may be symmetrical or asymmetrical. They may be stylized or realistic. This gives the carver a wide range for expression. In fact, there is hardly a form or design that cannot be adapted to chip carving.

When doing free-form designs, it is best to remember to vary the thickness of your cuts from chip to chip and even within the same chip. If all of your chips are the same size, the overall effect of the carving will be boring. By varying the thickness of your chips, you increase the shadow lines and give depth and dimension to your work.

Be bold and experimental in your designing. Many times just a hint of a flower, or leaf, or foliage will flow and pull a design together. Mixing geometric and free-form motifs is traditional and can produce some very exciting designs. The two forms complement each other. (Illus. 79–101)

Illus. 80. Wood buttons and pendants.

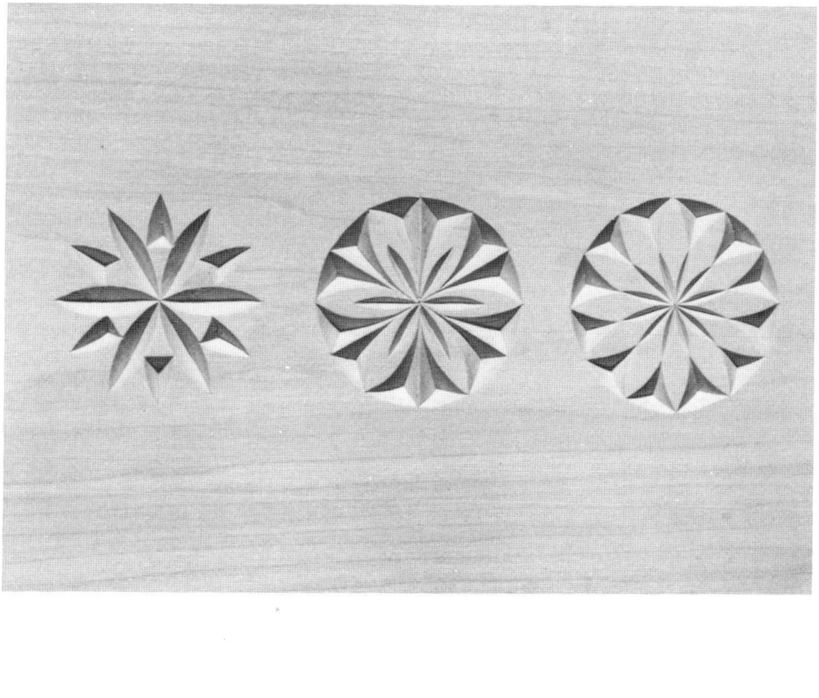

Illus. 81. Daisy design.

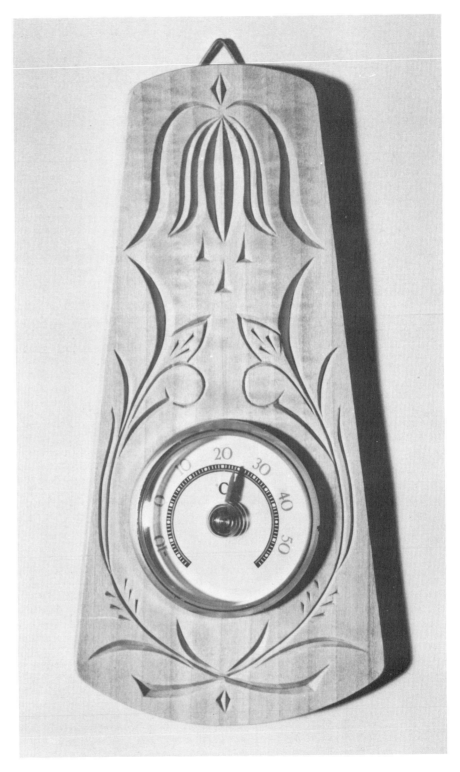

Illus. 82. Thermome-
ter.

Illus. 83. Tulip designs.

Illus. 84. Floral design.

Illus. 85. Chair back.

Illus. 86. Edelweiss.

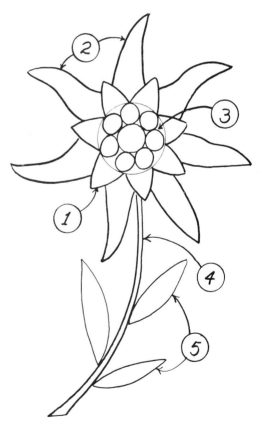

*Illus. 87. Edelweiss design showing
order for removing chips.*

Illus. 88. Floral design with first four measures of Verdi's "Requiem."

Illus. 89. Floral design with Old English lettering.

Illus. 90. Floral design.

Illus. 91. Cranes in flight.

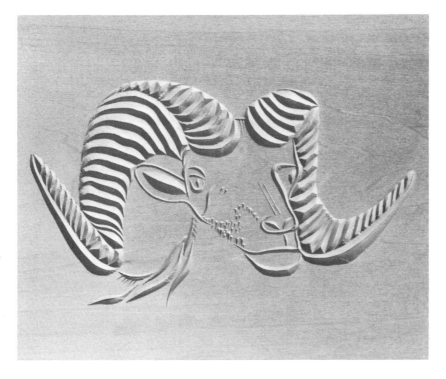

Illus. 92. Ram.

Illus. 93. Celtic cross.

Illus. 94. Lover's knot.

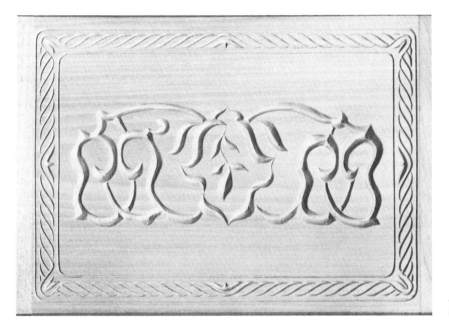

Illus. 95. Asymmetrical design.

Illus. 96. Logo of The Gate House, Ltd., Shreveport, Louisiana.

Illus. 97. Gothic design pattern.

Illus. 98. Gothic design.

Illus. 99. Double eagle from the House of Hapsburg.

Illus. 100. American Bald Eagle.

Illus. 101. Butter board.

LETTERING

Lettering has always been an integral part of chip carving. From a single intricate initial carved on a small jewelry box to complete poems, quotations, and mottos carved in huge letters on the exterior walls of houses, lettering gives the carver an unparalleled opportunity to personalize his work and express his feelings. Letters may even be incorporated as part of the design itself.

When doing lettering where more than one letter is used, it may be helpful to first use tracing paper when copying; or graph paper if you are going to draw the letters. This will allow you to get the proper spacing of the letters. Then, using pencil carbon paper, you can transfer your lettering directly onto the wood. Remember not to press too hard when transferring. It will make any necessary clean-up much easier.

Roman. Roman letters are extremely legible and may be used well with most designs. It is common to use all capitals when working with Roman lettering. Because it is best to remove the largest chips first, as in all chip carving, the following step-by-step method illustrates how this is easily accomplished. (Illus. 102)

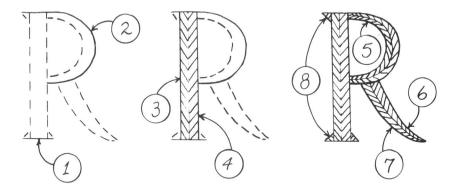

1. Make cut 1 to include the serifs, and cut 2. This will give you the end cuts of the largest chip.
2. Make cuts 3 and 4, relieving the largest chip.
3. Make cut 5 relieving the upper curved section and 6 and 7, relieving the remaining leg.
4. Cut the serifs, 8, last to complete the letter. (Illus. 103–110)

Old English. Old English lettering is very strong and bold. Because of its ornate style, the capital letters show very well as initials. But it is too ornate in most instances to use only capitals in full words. It is generally best to use both upper and lower cases when carving names and words. (Illus. 111–124)

Script. Script lettering is a very fancy and flowing style that can blend nicely with a similar design or be an actual part of it. Script also is probably the best style of lettering to use in creating monograms. When making a monogram, you will find that each letter fits into each of the others a little bit differently. That is, *A* fits together with *B* differently than it does with *C* or *D*. This means that when you design a monogram, you may have to alter each letter slightly in order that the whole monogram has an artistic flow to it. Because the letters of a good monogram will intersect each other several times, take special care not to insert the cutting knife any deeper than necessary. This will prevent lifting out the wood you want to remain, giving your work a clean, crisp appearance. (Illus. 125–140)

Illus. 102A

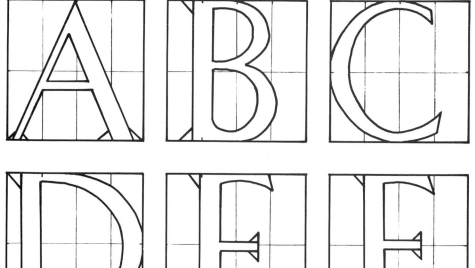
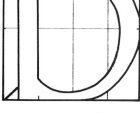
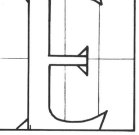
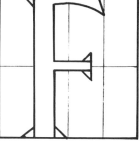

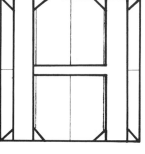
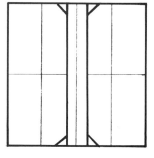
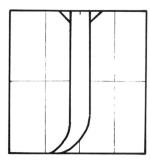
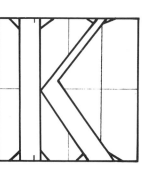
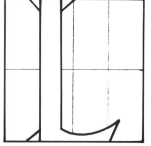

Illus. 103

Illus. 104

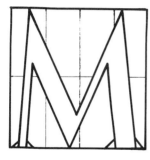
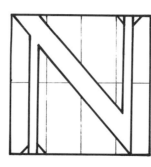
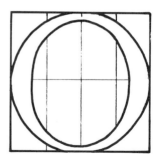

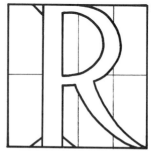

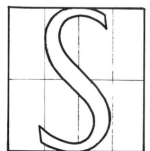
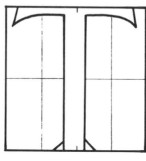
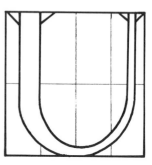

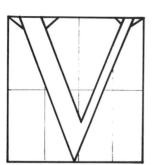
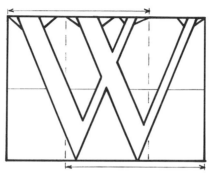

Illus. 105

Illus. 106

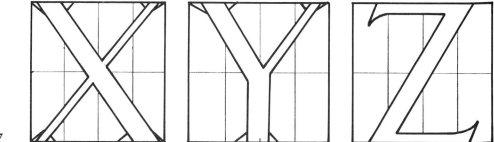

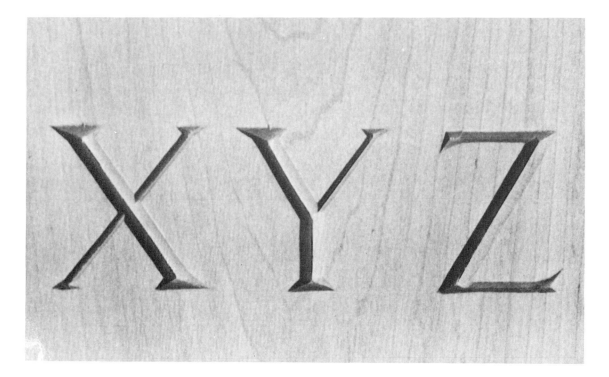

Illus. 108

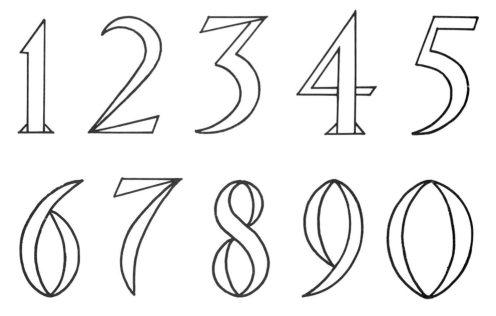

Illus. 109

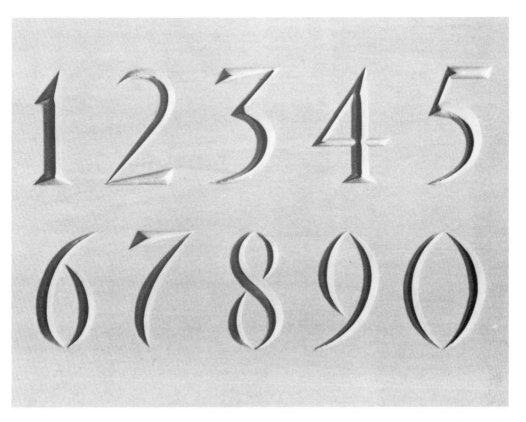

Illus. 110

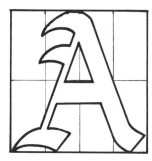  

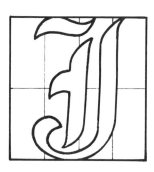  

Illus. 111

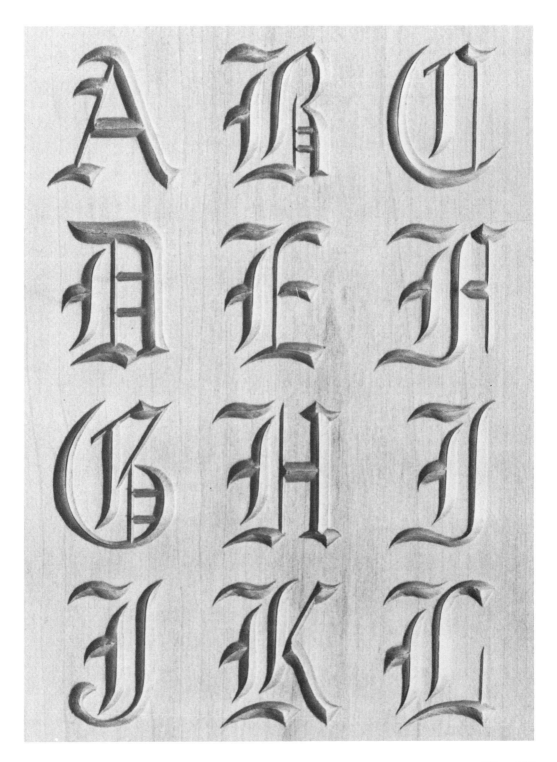

Illus. 112

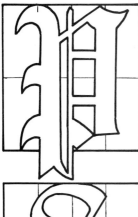  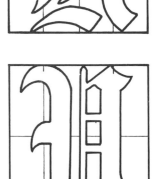

Illus. 113

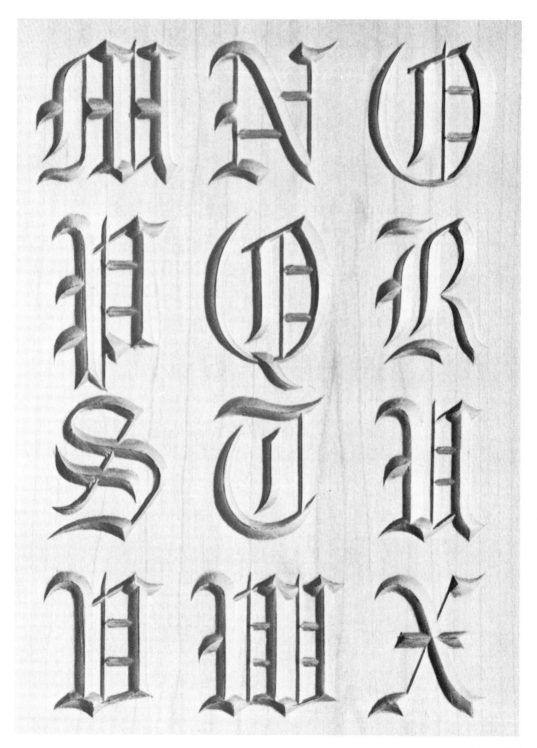

Illus. 114

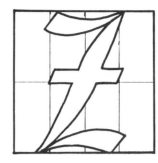
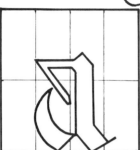
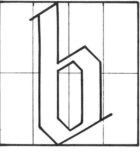
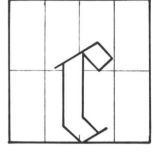
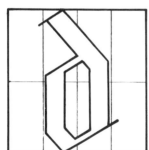
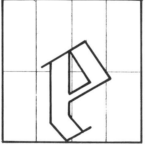
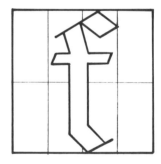
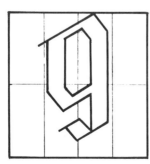
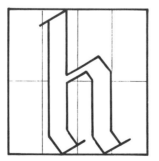
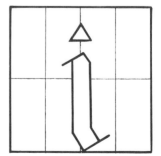

Illus. 115

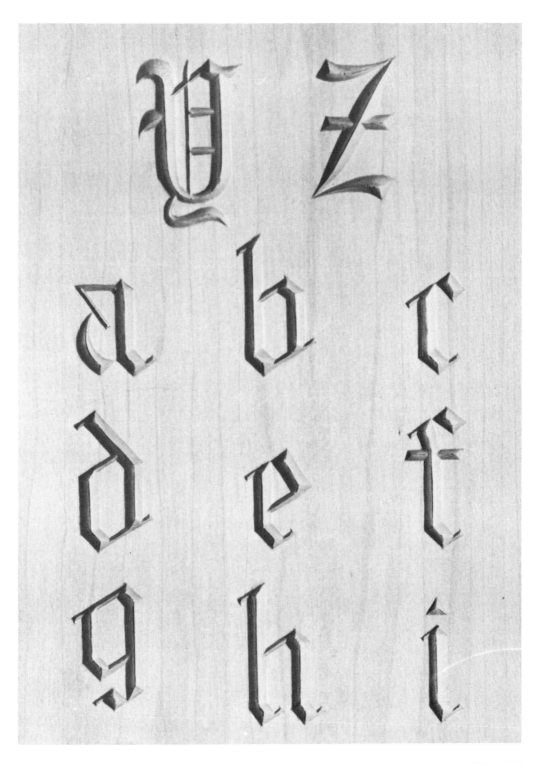

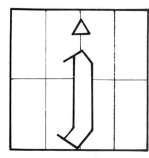 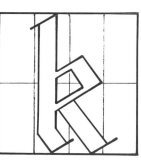 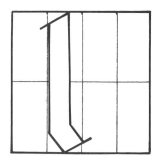

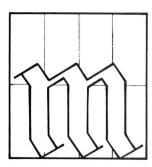 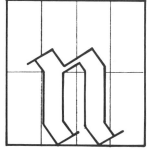 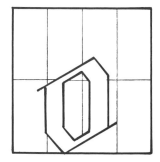

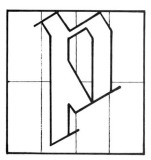 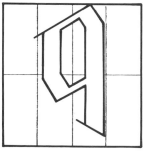 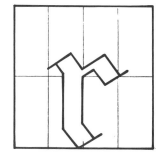

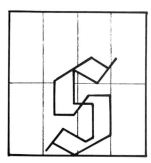 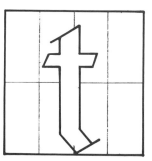 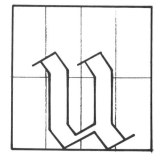

Illus. 117

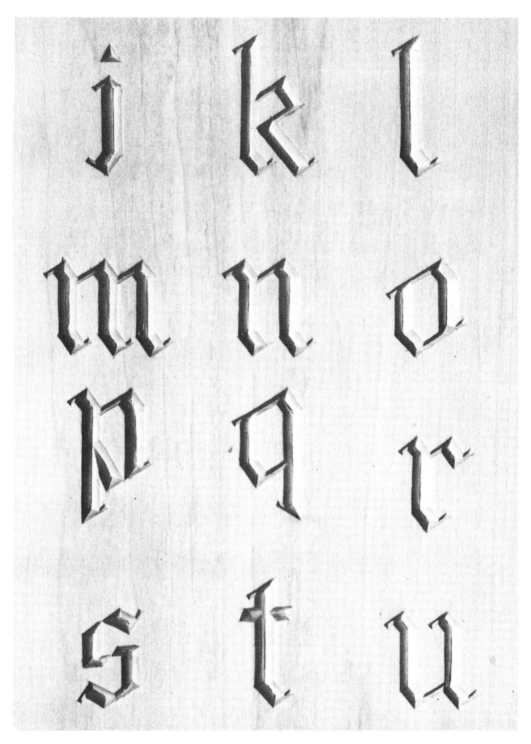

Illus. 118

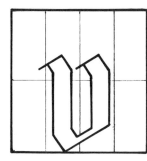 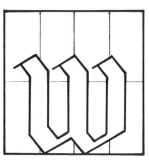 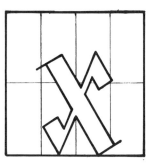

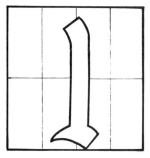 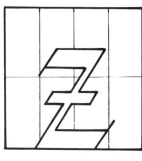

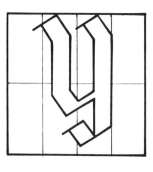 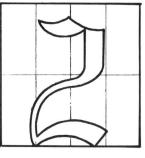 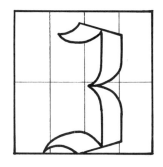

 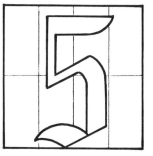 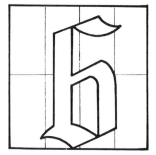

Illus. 119

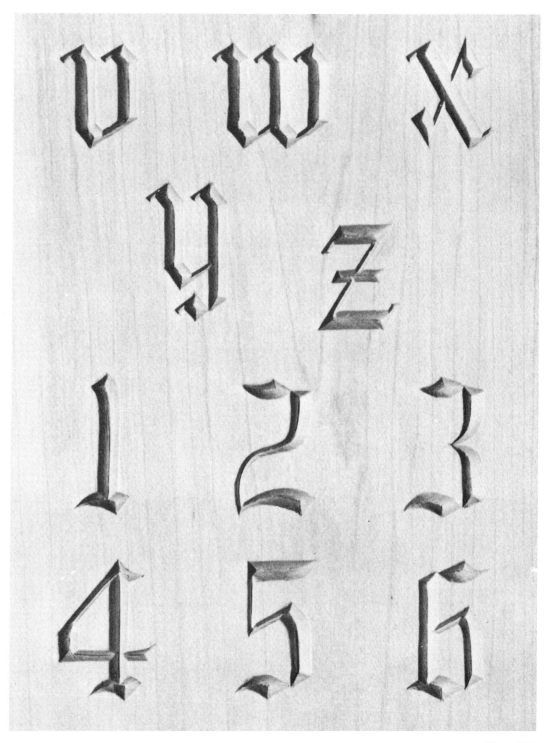

Illus. 120

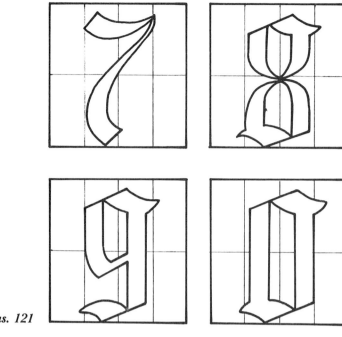

Illus. 121

Illus. 122

Illus. 123

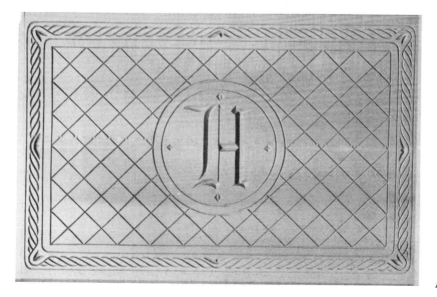

Illus. 124

  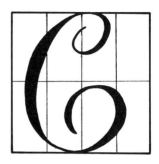

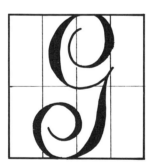 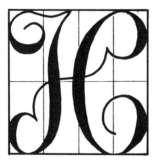 

  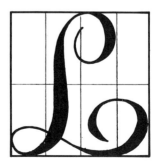

Illus. 125

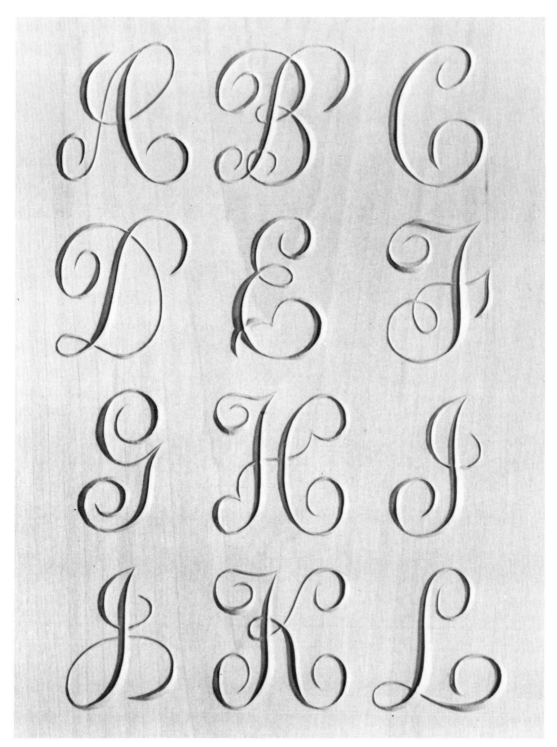

Illus. 126

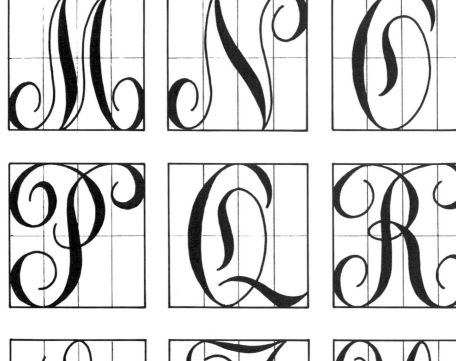

Illus. 127

Illus. 128

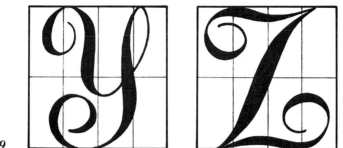

Illus. 129

Illus. 130

Illus. 131

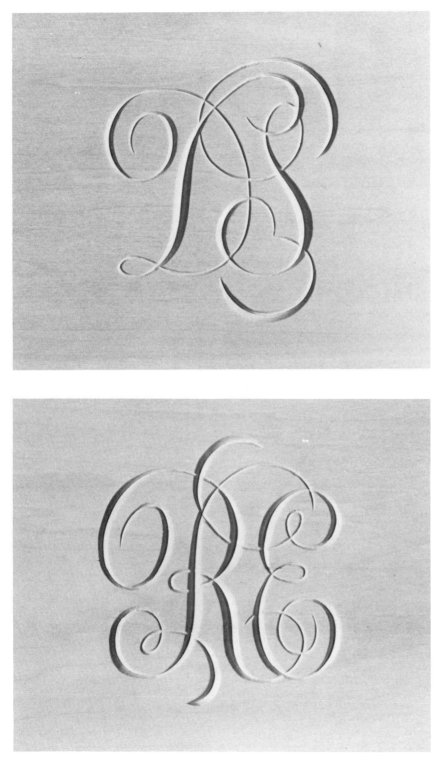

Illus. 132

Illus. 133

Illus. 134

Illus. 135

Illus. 136

Illus. 137

Illus. 138

Illus. 139

Illus. 140

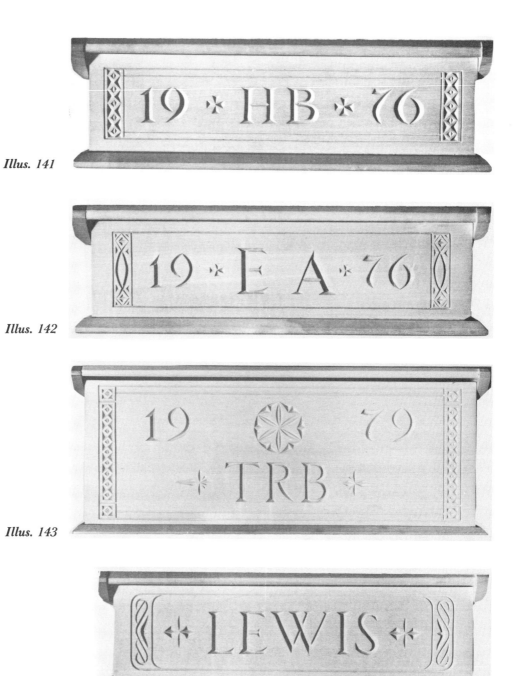

Illus. 141

Illus. 142

Illus. 143

Illus. 144

Illus. 145

Illus. 146

Illus. 147

Illus. 148

CLEANING AND FINISHING

It is inevitable that you will have some pencil lines or marks from carbon paper left on your work when you are finished carving. If you use a soft lead such as grade B and don't press hard when making your layout, removing all lines and marks will be much easier. A soft rubber eraser will remove your pencil marks. To remove the marks left by carbon paper, use an ink eraser. Care should be taken when erasing marks left on carved ridges as they may be delicate and could break off if handled too roughly.

When all the lines and marks have been removed, lightly sand the finished work with 220 grit sandpaper. This will freshen up the entire surface and prepare it for finishing. Always sand in the direction of the grain. When sanding be careful not to flatten any carved ridges in your work. This will take the crispness out of its appearance.

It is recommended that you finish your work because finishing will prevent fingerprints and dirt accumulating over a period of time, and will give you a surface that can be safely dusted and cleaned without harming the wood.

There are several ways to finish your work. With few exceptions, you will get most satisfying results with a natural finish rather than staining. This is particularly true when using basswood as it does not take most stains very well. If you do stain, it is best to test the stain first on a scrap piece of wood.

An excellent natural finish can be achieved with a dull (not satin or gloss) polyurethane. It is durable, flexible, easy to clean, and will give basswood a warm, honey color You should spray rather than brush. Because chip carving is incised, brushing has a tendency to fill your carving, making it difficult to get a smooth and crisp finish. Rather, spray on three to five thin coats uniformly. Allow the finish to dry thoroughly and sand lightly between coats using 220 grit sandpaper. On the last coat, make sure the surface is dust free before you spray. Do not sand after the last coat. Spray cans of dull polyurethane are easy to use and can be purchased at nearly any hardware dealer.

Illus. 150. Pine chest dated 1449.

HISTORICAL PICTURES

The test of an idea or design is how well it survives through the years. It's called tradition. The tradition of Kerbschnitzen or chip carving in Switzerland, shown here, goes back more than five hundred years. As you can see, many of the design ideas and motifs have not changed through the centuries. These uncommon antiques, carved by common men with artistic vision, speak well for the art, its followers, and its tradition.

The historical photographs in this section were taken in Brienz, Bern, Thun Castle, Spiez Castle, and the Simmental Valley in Switzerland.

Illus. 151. Jewelry box dated 1546.

Illus. 152. Jewelry box dated 1546.

Illus. 153. Jewelry box dated 1546.

Illus. 154. Side panel of pine chest dated 1528.

Illus. 155. Milking stool dated 1780.

Illus. 156. Chair, 18th century.

Illus. 157. Milking stool dated 1711.

Illus. 158. Small box dated 1658.

Illus. 159. Butter mould with initials F.B. dated 1813.

Illus. 160. Bread board dated 1762.

Illus. 161. Cheese board dated 1743.

Illus. 162. Chair with initials DM dated 1727.

Illus. 163. Small box, 17th century.

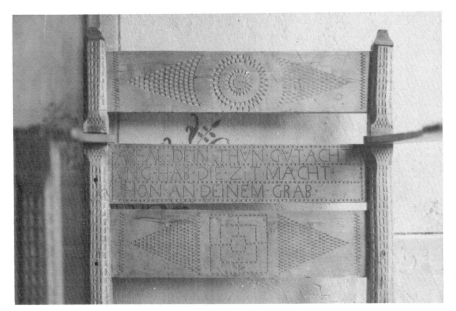

Illus. 164. Chair, 18th century.

Illus. 165. Chair back dated 1742.

Illus. 166. Bread board dated 1744.

Illus. 167. Butter carrier dated 1797.

Illus. 168. Butter carrier dated 1740.

Illus. 169. Butter carrier dated 1782.

Illus. 170. Butter carrier dated 1790.

Illus. 171. Ladle dated 1733.

Illus. 172. Water bucket with spout dated 1718.

Illus. 173. Ladle, 18th century.

Index

About the Author

Wayne Barton is an American-born professional woodcarver who presently resides outside Chicago in Park Ridge, Illinois, U.S.A. with his Swiss wife, Marlies, and their four children, Blaise, Teak, Cleve, and Heidi.

At first interested in woodcarving at the age of five by his Norwegian grandfather, he has had a serious interest in, and love for, carving all his life.

Mr. Barton took his formal training in Brienz, Switzerland and his work has been exhibited throughout Europe and North America. He is the founder and director of the Alpine School of Woodcarving.

Although he is versed in all disciplines of carving, Wayne Barton specializes in "Kerbschnitzen" or chip carving and has won both national and international awards and recognition for his work.

Acknowledgments

This book is the culminant effort of many people both directly and indirectly, to all of whom I am most grateful. What one gains through the years from the friendship and unselfish considerations of others is immeasurable. Gottlieb Brandli has been one such friend. He is a Swiss cabinetmaker of unequalled skill who has graciously shared with me much of his time and experience. Besides hand-selecting and drying all my wood, he has made many of the wood articles seen within these pages.

Studying under the knowledgeable and skilful guidance of my teacher, Emmi Wyler, of Brienz, Switzerland is an experience I shall cherish always. In the same way, the patience exhibited by my own students has allowed me to learn much from them also. Each has truly enriched me more than I have them.

I am indebted to those who physically contributed to putting this book together: Brian Fabbri for producing the photographs; Chung S. Yoo for his assistance and ideas for design and artwork; Joanne Inda for her very capable typing; and my sons, Blaise and Teak, for their erudite proofreading and notions of composition and context.

I also have been blessed with the warm friendship of many excellent carvers. In particular, I should like to mention Claude Michaelson and Roi Tauer. Their suggestions and sound judgments have helped chart the course to steer through this endeavor.

Most of all, it has been the constant loving support and understanding of my wife, Marlies, that have inspired me in this undertaking. Her keen artistic perception, fresh viewpoints and sage advice, upon which I have come to depend, have enabled me to see far beyond my own vision. It must therefore be openly acknowledged that this book is as much a product of her own energies and abilities as it is of mine. Without her persistent encouragement and faith, all that follows would never have been possible.